Bob Marley

Island Prophet

Mitchell Uscher

Ariel Books

**Andrews McMeel
Publishing**

Kansas City

www.andrewsmcmeel.com

photography © Adrian Boot

ISBN: 0-7407-0056-1

Library of Congress Catalog Card Number: 99-60625

contents

The story of Bob Marley is one of legend.

Marley grew up a poor, fatherless boy in the slums of Jamaica, yet he had the talent, vision, and courage to become the foremost superstar of reggae music. Always mindful of the poverty and hard times of the world he came from, Marley's songs of faith, hope, rebellion, and determination have brought inspiration and joy to audiences everywhere.

But Bob Marley was more than a magnificent musician. He was also a

Bob Marley

spiritual and political force in his native Jamaica and around the world. Although he died much too young at the age of thirty-six, Marley's music continues to bring his message of love and the unity of all people to a new generation of listeners.

February 6, 1945

Robert Nesta Marley is born in Nine Miles, Jamaica. He is the son of Norval Sinclair Marley, a white English army captain, and Cedella Booker, a Jamaican country girl. (Although most reliable sources say that Marley was born on February 6, the birth date on his passport read: April 6, 1945.)

1945-1957

Marley's father leaves the baby and mother and is rarely seen again. Bob

grows up a smart, healthy boy, and, for the most part, he enjoys his boyhood in the pretty country-side of the island.

1957-1960

At the age of twelve, Bob moves with his mother to a poor area of Kingston, the capital of Jamaica. As a teenager in the early 1960s, Marley, like many other children of the ghetto, is excited by the

Bob Marley

types of new music that are emerging from the streets of the city. These sounds will soon evolve into the global phenomenon called *reggae*.

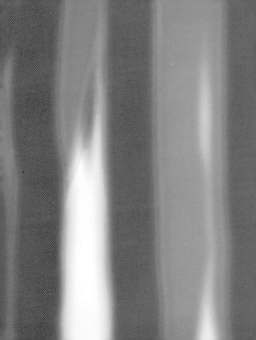

1961

Marley is sixteen years old when he forms his first harmony group, which then evolves into his first band. At first, the group is called The Rude Boys, but they are eventually known as The Wailers.

In addition to Bob Marley, the original Wailers include his friends Peter Tosh (born Winston McIntosh), Bunny Wailer (born Neville Livingston), Junior Braithwaite, and Beverly Kelso.

Bob Marley

1962

Bob flops with his first recording, a song called "Judge Not" (in fact, the song is credited to Bob *Morley!*). It is followed up with "One Cup of Coffee" and "Terror," but neither tune makes it to the charts.

1964

"Simmer Down" is the first hit for Bob Marley and the Wailers. Aimed at their rebellious peers, the record sells a very impressive eighty thousand copies. It is followed by, among others, "It Hurts to Be Alone," "I Am Going Home," "Mr. Talkative," "Rude Boy," "Lonesome Feeling," and "I'm Still Waiting."

Although the group's popularity grows in Jamaica with the release of its first album, *The Wailing Wailers*, Marley and the band barely make enough money to survive.

Bob Marley

1966

Marley marries Rita Anderson on February 10. Born Alpharita Constantia Anderson, she is a singer too, formerly with the group the Soulettes.

Soon after the wedding, Marley moves to Delaware in the United States for about eight months. He works many odd jobs, including one on an assembly line

in a Chrysler automobile plant, but decides to return to Jamaica.

1968-1969

The Wailers continue recording but meet with limited success, so Marley starts writing songs for such other recording stars as Johnny Nash.

1969-1971

Marley becomes a committed Rastafarian, letting his hair grow out in dreadlocks as part of his devotion to the movement. He also records on his newly formed Tuff Gong label with the Wailers, but their albums are not big sellers outside of Jamaica.

Jamaica: Multifaceted Jewel

Jamaica, Bob Marley's homeland, is an island of unsurpassed beauty. With its glorious beaches, majestic mountains, and pristine blue sky, it has been a jewel of the Caribbean for centuries. However, Jamaica has also had a surprisingly tumultuous history for such a gorgeous island gem.

Discovered by Columbus in 1494, it was the pirate center of the world during the 1600s. A massive earthquake in 1692 sent part of the island to the bottom of the sea. During its history, sugar, bananas, and bauxite

Bob Marley

have been major industries of the island.

First under Spanish, then British rule, Jamaica became an independent nation on August 6, 1962. But turmoil still raged on the island as opposing political groups fought for power. Even though he was a musical artist, Marley's socially conscious songs made him a political target. This was because Bob Marley and the Wailers reached unprecedented levels of popularity and influence in Jamaica, and Marley's opinions on issues were given the

weight and attention that are usually reserved for political or religious leaders.

Now on the verge of the twenty-first century, Jamaica has a newfound prosperity and peace—a peace Bob Marley hoped for and worked for throughout his short life.

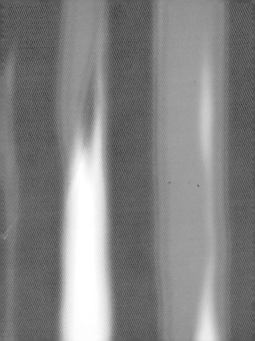

The
Roots of
Reggae

Reggae initially developed in the 1950s, when Jamaican musicians combined the indigenous folk music of the island with other musical forms such as jazz, African sounds, and New Orleans rhythm and blues.

Reggae music is known for its unique and hypnotic rhythms as well as for its politically and socially relevant lyrics, which often include themes of Rastafarianism, racial pride, and the tumultuous nature of Jamaican life. The songs tell of the troubles, joys, and dreams of the downtrodden, trying to escape the slums of Jamaica.

Bob Marley is *the* giant figure in reggae music, and his socially compassionate songs are the standard by which all of reggae is—and will be—measured.

Marley's style is a blend of rock 'n' roll, rhythm and blues, soul, and Jamaican folk music. His work often has a lighter touch, which makes it accessible to a much wider audience, but those jaunty rhythms

often belie the stinging lyrics that speak of prejudice, power, and war.

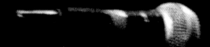

Reggae remains an important component of the contemporary music scene and has had a major influence on other forms of popular music, including rap.

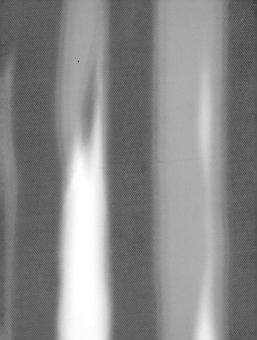

The Rasta Way

Bob Marley was strongly devoted to Rastafarianism, which was brought to Jamaica by American black nationalist leader Marcus Garvey (1887–1940). It preaches the divinity of Haile Selassie of Ethiopia, denounces white domination, and advocates a return of black people to Africa, particularly to Ethiopia.

In Rastafarianism, Haile Selassie (whose family name was Ras Tafari) is considered the personification of God (Jah); it is believed that one day, Selassie will return to lead his people

Bob Marley

back to Africa (a subject Marley sang about in his 1977 hit, "Exodus: Movement of Jah People").

Rastafarian men like Marley grow their hair in long, plaited dreadlocks. They also wear woolen caps that are colored green (for the land of Ethiopia), yellow (for the sun), black (for their skin), and red (for the blood of their brothers). Rastafarian women cover their heads, use no makeup, and wear long, modest-looking clothing. The use of marijuana (also known as "ganja") has a place of religious prominence

in the Rastafari movement.

Marley's conversion to Rastafarianism greatly influenced both his music and his attitude toward life. In fact, his religion often became the subject of his songs and his reggae music became the medium through which he presented the ideals of Rastafarianism to the world.

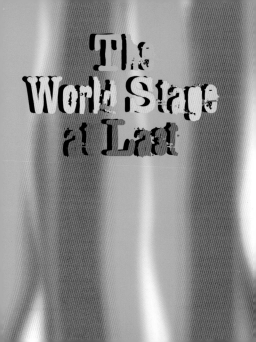

The
World Stage
at Last

1972

Bob Marley and the Wailers are signed by Chris Blackwell, the founder of Island Records, who hopes to break both the group and reggae music into the international market. Their debut record for the label, "Catch a Fire," is the group's first album to be released in the United States. With a strong promotional push by Island Records, Marley's popularity begins to spill over into mainstream pop.

1973

Bob Marley and the Wailers are dropped as an opening act for Sly and the Family Stone's U.S. tour, supposedly for upstaging the main act with their energy and talent. In concert, Marley always gives his all, constantly dancing as he plays and sings, sweat-soaked from the exertion. Many say that Marley gets so involved during his performances that he often seems to be in a higher, trancelike state.

Bob Marley

In 1973, both Peter Tosh and Bunny Livingston leave the Wailers to start their own solo careers. They are replaced, in part, by the I-Threes, a female backup vocal group featuring Bob's wife Rita, Judy Mowatt, and Marcia Griffiths. Griffiths will later have a hit record of her own called "Electric Boogie," which helps to create the dance sensation known as the Electric Slide.

1974

Eric Clapton tops the U.S. charts with his version of Bob Marley's song, "I Shot the Sheriff." This cover becomes a hit all over the globe.

1975

Bob Marley has his own international breakthrough in popularity with his album *Natty Dread*. The record reaches ninety-two on the U.S. charts, and a song from the album, "No Woman, No Cry," becomes a reggae classic.

Bob Marley

Marley's album *Rastaman Vibrations* hits number eight in the United States and spends twenty-two weeks on the charts. A single from that album, "Roots Rock Reggae," hits fifty-one, making it the only Marley single to appear on the American charts. Another song from the album, "War," has powerful lyrics taken from a speech by Haile Selassie.

December 3, 1976

Just before Marley is to give a free,

government-sponsored concert in Kingston, a group of gunmen force their way into Marley's home. Marley, Rita, and his manager Don Taylor are all shot, but they miraculously escape with their lives. It is never discovered if the assassination attempt was politically motivated or who the assailants are. Marley goes on to do the concert before eighty thousand cheering fans.

1977

While Marley's career success continues with his album *Exodus*, a number-

Bob Marley

twenty hit on the U.S. charts, there is concern about his physical health when one of his toes is removed because of a cancerous growth.

1978-1979

Increasingly popular with audiences around the world, Marley makes his first trip to Africa, including Kenya and Ethiopia, which he claims to be his spiritual homeland. Bob Marley's fame continues to grow; his group becomes the first reggae band to headline at the famed Apollo Theatre in Harlem.

1980

With increased dedication to Rastafarianism, Marley takes a new name: Berhane Selassie. He is also baptized at the Ethiopian Orthodox Church in Kingston, Jamaica. In December, Stevie Wonder has a hit with a tribute song to Marley titled "Master Blaster." By this time, Marley's fight with cancer has become public.

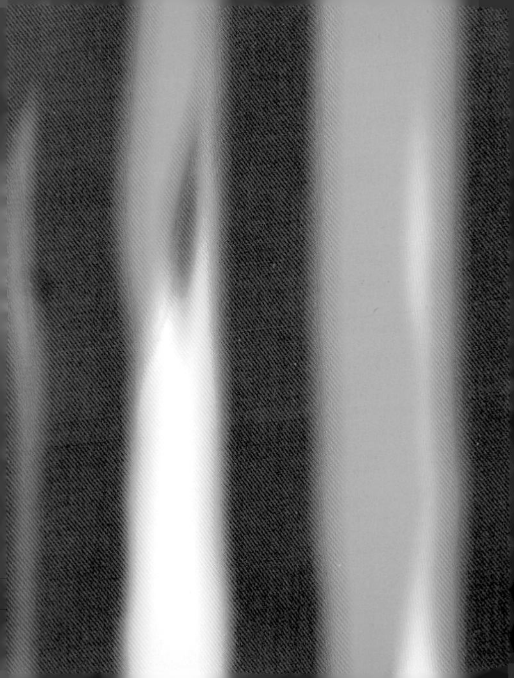

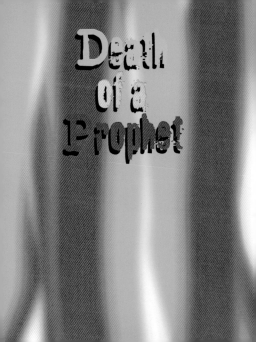

Death
of a
Prophet

October 8, 1980

While jogging in Central Park in New York City, Bob Marley collapses. As he is receiving radiation treatment for a brain tumor, his famed dreadlocks fall out. His wife, Rita, keeps the locks and has them made into a wig. (It is later placed on Bob's head in his coffin, which also includes his copy of the Bible and his guitar.)

After traveling to Germany for an experimental but futile cancer treatment, Marley tries to fly back home

Bob Marley

to Jamaica, but gets no farther than Miami.

May 11, 1981
At the age of thirty-six, Bob Marley dies of brain cancer. Marley's funeral service is held in Kingston's National Heroes Arena, then his body is taken to his hometown of Nine Miles. It is estimated that half of the island's citizens come to pay their respects, making it the most memorable day of mourning Jamaica has ever known.

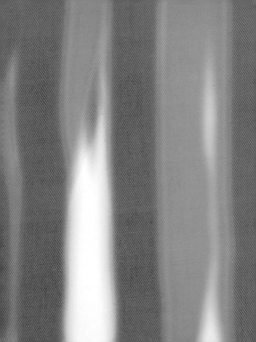

Reggae music . . . carry earth force, people rhythm . . . it is a rhythm of working people, movement, a music of the masses. . . .

Is better to die fighting for yar freedom than to be a prisoner all the days of yar life.

Money is *not* my richness. My richness is to live, and walk on the earth, and bear fruit.

Bob Marley

The system want pure love songs like ol' Frank Sinatra; they don't want not'ing wit' no protest. It makes too much trouble.

The Devil is very generous, mon— he'll give you everything for your soul!

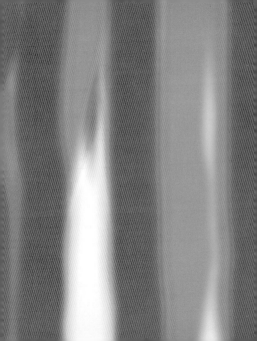

The
Legacy
of a
Legend

The popularity of Bob Marley and the influence of his music have only continued to grow since his death.

Marley's records still sell all over the globe. In fact, *Legend*, a posthumous collection of Marley's greatest hits, is the best-selling reggae album of all time. It has been on the best-selling pop catalog album charts for an incredible five hundred weeks!

And the honors accorded to Marley have only increased since his passing. In 1994, Bob Marley was posthumously inducted into the Rock and

Roll Hall of Fame. In Marley's homeland of Jamaica, where he is a national hero, a commemorative stamp was issued in his honor in 1982.

In 1990, Marley's birthday, February 6, was proclaimed a national holiday in that country. There is also a Bob Marley Museum in Kingston.

But Marley's most enduring legacy is the effect of his music on people all over the world. Marley sang to join people together, lift the downtrodden, and inspire everyone to work toward a better life. His songs express his vision of "one world, one love," a vision that transcends all racial, religious, and social barriers.

Book design and composition
by Diane Hobbing of
Snap-Haus Graphics
in Edgewater, NJ.

The type is set in Filosofia, Fragile,
and Passport Bold.